korkscrewed

EDITING
Brianne Cail, Paige McPhee

COCKTAIL ARTIST & MIXOLOGIST
Kris Bahamondes

COCKTAIL PHOTOGRAPHY
Elaine Fancy

HEADSHOT PHOTOGRAPHY
Emily Ferris

DESIGN
Olivia Rohner

Printed in the United States of America
Published by Gatekeeper Press
gatekeeperpress.com

gatekeeper press
Where Authors are Family

korkscrewed

by jordan quinn

*The
Cocktails & Confessions
of a
Modern Dating Girl*

To my parents, Mom & Daddy, there are no two people more dedicated to one another. Thank you for being my Xanax before a promising date & the glue gun for every broken heart.

I hope to one day find a love like yours.

contents

foreword

by paige mcphee

EVER SINCE I WAS 5 YEARS OLD, I've been a romantic.

I distinctly remember asking my kindergarten teacher how to spell *anonymous* so I could appropriately sign love letters to boys in my class. I used to share shy glances with kids across the classroom and write my first name with their last names in my journal. When we got a tad older, I would spend hours at my mom's old iMac, typing and deleting "Hey" to display names like HockeyBoy33 on MSN, or Skype crushes from camp. But love does not always favour romantics. In fact, sometimes growing up can be all the more awkward and painful as those with big hearts and bigger dreams try to find someone to give their affection to. I know I spent much of my adolescence on the sidelines, spilling my soul to my journal, blooming slowly while others opened up.

love, *in many ways* is like achieving the perfect buzz.

The author of this book, Jordan Quinn, much like myself, shared these anxieties and insecurities. As young women today we're constantly finding things to critique about ourselves, whether it's tits the size of Tic Tacs or a moustache that's much darker than peach fuzz. Falling in love, *or like*, is all the harder when you're still trying to love your own skin as it grows and changes. Puberty, peer pressure, and even paranoia can cause many a romantic roadblock—many of which Jordan will share in pages to come.

The best way to look at love, however, is not in a linear way.

It is in no way a race or a helpful Google Map, giving you step by step instructions on how to succeed. Love, in many ways, is like achieving the perfect buzz. Finding a drink that works for your lifestyle and taste. Something you can enjoy, alone or with company. Something to look forward to after a long day. The perfect drink takes time and effort. It takes a lot of trial and error, sampling sips that are sugary, bitter, tasteless or overwhelming, until you and your taste buds are exhausted. And, like any great thing, love arrives unexpectedly. Just like a drink sent across the room—it is refreshing, light and sweet. Korkscrewed follows Jordan through a night at the bar, as she tries to find not mister right—but a mister rosé.

cereal

dater

ingredients

1.5 oz	Angel's Envy Bourbon
.75 oz	Peanut Orgeat
2 oz	Peanut butter puffs Cereal Almond Milk
2 dash	Ms. Better's Bitters Miraculous Foamer

garnish

Peanut butter puffs

mixing instructions

In a mixing tin, add the Angel's Envy Bourbon, peanut orgeat cereal milk & foamer. Fill the tin with ice & shake, shake, shake, shake it vigorously to dilute and chill. Double strain cocktail into a chilled, small Collins glass. Garnish & enjoy.

Tipsy

Don't get tied down! This cocktail can be made with a wide variety of dry cereals. Simply infuse your almond milk with your favourite cereal! Garnish to taste.

dear

reader,

DURING MY TIME ON "THE APPS," dear reader, I decided that dating is a lot like eating an entire box of cereal. I had officially dated enough flakes and nuts and I was eager to find the prize.

If I was tired of being single, I was absolutely exhausted by dating—an unfortunate combination that left me equal parts irritated and inspired. Strangely inspired. So I decided to put pinot to pucker, and pen to paper. I wrote down every noteworthy and every cringeworthy moment of a year's worth of mistakes, headaches, and heartbreaks. And as I sketched my thoughts across an entire notebook, my tipsy words harmoniously began to read like Taylor Swift lyrics. In essence, I had crafted an album of exes and woes.

As I documented the details of the patterns that threatened to make me forever cynical towards love, I realized that modern dating ethos had led me to something greater than love at first swipe; it led me to Korkscrewed.

if anything, this book will only give you a hangover.

I poured the rest of the bottle in my glass, and the rest of my heart on the pages, and watched the very stories you're about to read write themselves. As I recalled the highs and lows of past Bumble dates, I giggled at my own mistakes and misfortunes. I toasted to the men that co-starred in the amusing reality that was my single life. They were the flakes and the nuts of my metaphorical cereal bowl, and the unnamed subjects of the pages that follow.

Whatever your relationship status, this book is for you. It's for those of us who at one point in time have had the wrong taste in men, but always the right taste in cocktails and wine. Perhaps you had your heart broken and you're lying in your bed of self-pity, feeling more useless than the *T* in pinot. Maybe you're the heartbreaker and—like a bull in a china shop—have shattered hearts like wine glasses and left men to pick up the pieces. Or you're in the wrong relationship, where that once strong connection has slowly grown weaker than public transit WiFi.

Korkscrewed: The Cocktails & Confessions of a Modern Dating Girl, is a series of dating revelations, anecdotes and awkward encounters that I have collected in my humble twenty–six years. Enclosed are the perfect cocktail pairings that have made each chapter of my dating life all the more bearable. These chapters were written in every stage of the dating game. From that first tipsy typing session to the published pages you're reading now, I have dated some *nuts*, kissed some *flakes*, and been convinced (once or twice) that I'd found my *prize*.

So I apologize, dear reader, if you have picked up this book in false hope that these Pepto-pink pages will cure your dating nausea—if anything, this book will only give you a hangover.

with wit
& wine.

jordan
xx

ingredients

1.5 oz	Bacardi Cuatro Rum
.5 oz	Coconut Cream
.75 oz	Lime Juice
.5 oz	Demerara Syrup
6-8	Fresh Mint Leaves
1 oz	Perrier

garnish

An edible flower & fresh mint sprigs

mixing instructions

Mix the Bacardi Cuatro, coconut cream, lime juice, Demerara Syrup & hand-clapped mint leaves. Fill the tin with ice & shake, shake, shake senora to dilute & chill. Double strain the cocktail into a collins glass over fresh ice. Top with Perrier, garnish & sip away.

Tipsy

Hosting a bachelorette or bridal shower? Add mint springs & an edible flower that match the bridal party's bouquets/corsages for a fun custom cocktail!

commit
mint *issues*

1

spit *swappin'*

I HAD MY FIRST KISS WHEN I WAS FIVE. It was shared with a boy named Nicky and satisfying the cliché of every young romance, he was, quite literally the boy next door.

Our love was as simple as the landscape in which it was harvested, Wheatland Avenue. We played at the purple park for the good slides and the yellow park for the good swings; we rode our bikes down our street, as far as our parents' view allowed; and on occasion, in the privacy of my backyard, Nicky would even agree to play house with me. A testament to our generation, we assumed our usual roles, Nick Carter and Geri Halliwell, when playing husband and wife.

And though an American boy band sensation and an iconic British pop star may have seemed a geographically incapable couple, such was not the case for this Ginger Spice and her Nicky Carter.

Nicky was six, and therefore cool, wise and desirable in my eyes. He was taller than the other boys on our street and the fastest on a two-wheel bike. He was the Wheatland Avenue stud and he was mine. All mine. I felt a sense of pride the day he took me by the hand in front of all the neighborhood kids and led me to this dad's garage. He placed his clammy hands on my chubby cheeks, pressed me against the car and kissed me. On. My. Lips. Just like the movies. Just like moms and dads.

but the *pride* was short lived.

But the pride was short lived.

My mother interrupted our seven seconds in heaven. She took me by the hand and led me back to our house. I blew Nicky a kiss over my shoulder. He caught it, pressed it against his lips and sent me off with a suggestive wink. *I'm a good kisser*, I confidently concluded.

What followed was nothing short of an unnecessary discussion about age-appropriate relationships. My mom's tone suggested minor disappointment, but the smirk she so unsuccessfully tried to mask, led me to believe she may have felt otherwise. *But he kissed me*, I still retorted — a rationalization that would echo back at me on the playground, just days later, when I caught a classmate locking lips with my other boyfriend. My school boyfriend.

His name was Liam. A stark contrast to Nicky, Liam was short and blonde and had an obsession with drawing tattoos on himself. Thoughtful girlfriend that I am, I gave him one of my coloured markers for his birthday. We never made it to first base. But he was simply a school-day distraction; Someone to keep me occupied between the hours of 9 a.m. and 3 p.m., until I returned home to Nicky. Permanent or not, it would have been hard to sell my dad on Liam's inked sleeve, anyway.

To my parents' relief my mini-make out session with Nicky would be the last of my premature promiscuities. The sexual display was hardly foreshadowing of any teenage angst and recklessness to come. In fact, my lips would remain lonely for over a decade thereafter.

My next kiss was shared with a crush two years my senior. He was one of the popular guys in our school but like most of my post-pubescent relationships, this one moved at a glacial pace. We smiled at each other in the hall when I was a freshman, exchanged numbers when I was a sophomore, and made plans to hang out when I was a junior.

He was away at university and had returned home for Christmas the night he suggested I stop by his friend's for a drink. I panicked. Invite or not, my wingwoman Sarah and I had absolutely no business being at a university party.

But a Red Solo Cup of liquid courage and a shot of teenage invincibility was the signature, underage, cocktail that led us to that basement beer pong tournament.

Sarah, like most all of my other friends, had already lost her kissing virginity. I bore witness to the highly anticipated event a year earlier, at our sophomore semi-formal. She and her then boyfriend swapped spit and swayed in their coordinated purple semi-formal wear, while the rest of us, perverted on-lookers, pointed and high-fived. Despite what all the movies suggested would happen, their braces did not interlock.

I had hoped for something equally romantic when my time came. To my advantage (I thought) I had my friends' culminated experiences and advice to reference to make the moment all the more magical.

"Just draw the ABC's with your tongue," they would say.

But when the opportunity arose, on that December night, my mind drew a complete blank. Instead, in the back room of that basement, my VEX soaked tongue just laid flaccid in my crush's mouth, likely drowning any possibility of us living happily ever after. Despite the tsunami I just inflicted in his mouth, he kindly walked our underage asses home. He and I would stop every few steps to kiss under the falling snowflakes, while a drunk Sarah would point and cheer in the same obnoxious manner that I had for her, just a year earlier.

We said goodnight and I stumbled the last few feet to my front door. Turning to close the door quietly behind me, he sent me off with a smile and familiar wink. *Immaasd still a goodf kissder*, I slurred to myself, as I wiped the excess saliva from the corners of my mouth.

just

draw

the

abc's

with your

tongue.

rose-bud

ingredients

1.5 oz	Rose-infused Grey Goose
.5 oz	Martini Riserva Speciale Bitter
1 tbsp	Rhubarb preserves
.5 oz	simple syrup
.75 oz	lemon juice
1.5 oz	Perrier

garnish

Clothespinned edible flower

mixing instructions

In a mixing tin add the rose-infused Grey Goose, Martini Riserva Speciale Bitter & rhubarb preserves. Stir the preserves into the spirits to blend them evenly. Add the simple syrup & lemon juice to the tin before filling it with ice. Shake vigorously to dilute and chill. Double strain into a large rocks glass over fresh ice, garnish & nip… I mean sip!

Tipsy

Invest in mini clothespins! They'll elevate the simplest of cocktails & allow you to get creative with your garnishing. Hosting a girls night? Use the clothespins & garnishes to customize each guest's glass. Always essential to mark your territory… Am I right?

2

itty bitty titty pity *part 1*

IN ALL MATTERS OF COMING INTO WOMANHOOD, I arrived fashionably late.

My boobs remained rosebuds, while those around me fully blossomed. An emergency package of pads collected dust until I turned a surprising seventeen. And until the ripe age of nineteen, the only penises I had ever seen were those sketched in my biology and *Fully Alive* textbooks.

Layer by layer, piece by piece I will expose—through Korkscrewed—the misfortunes of my adolescent late comings; but only in the same painfully slow manner that it took for me to graduate puberty.

The greatest difference between graduating from school versus puberty is in the reversed grading rubric. While A's were the benchmark for report card success, an A in cup size marked a personal fail that was so poignantly public.

The summer before high school, I so desperately longed to fill out a bathing suit top with the same perfection as my best friend, Brianne. With my hair in an unflattering bob at the time, I looked like her confused younger brother when we laid poolside. Though she would complain of occasional back pains and other discomforts, the physical ailments of being blessed in the chest, I thought, must pale in comparison to the emotional wreckage my flatness evoked.

When I was in eighth grade, a class photo circulated our homeroom. Written across each of my classmates was a word that two culprits thought best described us all. It was, in essence, a St. Bernard Burn Book. When the photo came to me, the letters F-L-A-T were scrambled across my chest. Hardly a cryptic message. The sentiment read loud and clear.

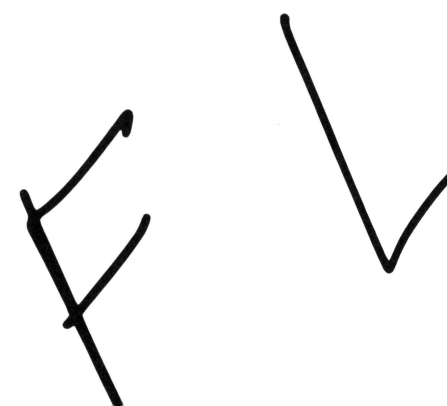

My boobs, or lack thereof, had been recognized, publicized and criticized. I left school that day humiliated, my entire self reduced to four offensive letters. I ran to my room, in a fit of pre-pubescent rage and I slammed my door behind me. In the privacy of my own room, I stared self-loathing at my pouting reflection and sad excuse for breasts. To make matters worse, a quarter turn to the right showed no signs of a blossoming bum either.

Or so I thought. Little did I know that those A's would become E's, and in a few year's time not only would I graduate from puberty, but I'd be earning extra credit.

ingredients

1.5 oz	D'usse VSOP
.5 oz	Martini Riserva Speciale Ambrato
.5 oz	Vanilla bean syrup
3 dash	Angostura bitters

garnish

AConfidence & attitude

mixing instructions

In a mixing glass add the D'usse VSOP, Martini Riserva Speciale Ambrato, vanilla bean syrup & Angostura bitters. Fill the mixing glass with ice & stir the cocktail to chill. Strain the cocktail into a large rocks glass over a Single XL sphere of ice, ice, baby.

Tipsy

This is a STRONG drink made for a STRONG woman! Aka YOU! Enjoy, boss lady. You deserve it.

d cup

itty bitty titty pity *part 2*

IN THE PARISIAN INSPIRED DRESSING ROOM, I waited for Mae—a sales associate at Victoria's Secret, with proportionate breasts of her own—to return with a selection of bras in my new, big-girl size.

32E.

I moved and posed in every angle, in a light that made the palest of flesh seem perfectly sun-kissed, revelling in the fact that my boobs clapped together when I jumped up and down.

full on.
womanly.
adult.

There it is, I thought. The round of applause I deserved. I did, after all, grow them myself.

Even without direct exposure to sunlight, my teenage rosebuds, overwatered with prayers and overfed by snack bar cheesy bread, had actually blossomed into breasts.

Full on. Womanly. Adult. Breasts.

Late as I was to cross the puberty finish line, any conversations of "size" amongst my girlfriends had far shifted from our own female bodies. Thus my cleavage, in all its perky glory, was old news and overshadowed by the varying sexcapades of my less uptight friends.

So with a celebratory pat on the back, I welcomed myself into womanhood.

breasts.

But the thrills of being so blessed in the chest were short-lived. Always struggling to get on the same page, one boob forever seemed to pour out the front of every tank top, the other, the side of every bathing suit. Alas, my over-sized boobs quickly became public enemies number one and two.

Mae returned with the holy trinity of basic and boring bras: a cotton balconette in black, a cotton demi in white, and a full-coverage cotton number in a hue that can only be described as band-aid beige. I watched my expression fade from excitement to exhaustion as I struggled to fasten myself into each harness. I caught myself staring in the mirror, self-loathing, just as I had a few years earlier. This time, however, I sported a beige, full-coverage contraption that was sure to keep both my boobs and virginity intact.

"Now this, Victoria," I thought, "is something I'd like to keep a secret."

main
squeeze

ingredients

1 oz	Martini Riserva Speciale Bitter
3 oz	Martini sparkling rose'
1.5 oz	Grapefruit juice
1 oz	Perrier

garnish

Trimmed lemon zest

mixing instructions

In a chilled flute or champagne glass, add the Martini
Riserva Speciale Bitter, Martini Rose', grapefruit juice &
Perrier. Stir the ingredients gently to mix, garnish &
Enjoy.

(Tip)sy

When life gives you lemons (or grapefruit) be sure
to add some zest to this cocktail! For a little extra
citrus try different Perrier flavors, like lemon,
grapefruit, or even strawberry.

4

sarah

I HAVE A DOLL NAMED SARAH.

She has hardly left my grip since the day I was born. Now, having both just passed the quarter-of-a-century mark, I hope I've aged better than her.

Her once pink dress has turned a questionably dark hue, her bonnet hangs sadly by three tiny threads and her torn cotton flesh now reveals the stuffing within. For years my grandma has led the "clean Sarah" crusade.

Always offering to sew her, begging to wash her, and threatening to throw her away. And so, in more recent years, I've kept Sarah *far* from my grandma's reach. I fear a spin in the washer, even the delicate cycle would be a death sentence for her now frail frame.

My friends also voice their disgust for Sarah. In their words she is what "nightmares are made of". And so, growing up, sleepover invitations were often contingent upon my promise to leave my thunder buddy at home. After negotiating the conditions of the overnight offer, Sarah and I, more often than not, would stay home in protest.

My childhood friend, also named Sarah, has never found flattery in sharing her name with my doll. Sarah has never been too couth to diagnose my doll as diseased, and me as chronically single, should I continue the codependent relationship. It pangs me to admit my friend's points were validated by way of my virginity's shelf life — a shelf life, which to most Western Mustangs, may be comparable to that of a can of soup. Nonperishable.

Don't get me wrong, the underage freshman of my residence weren't exactly lining up to get with me. I wore sports bras to the club, abused the midnight snack bar, and had yet to determine my alcohol tolerance, all of which hardly rendered me Western's most eligible bachelorette.

But as it turns out, a faceless doll also does little for a girl's budding love life.

Framed by throw pillows and empty vodka bottles, on my dorm room bed sat Sarah. She was a centerpiece of the room and a hot topic of conversation with most visitors. When they'd come for a visit, I'm sure my parents rejoiced at the sight of Sarah, as though the doll to which I had grown nose-blind to likely warded off any non-catholic university activity. And they were right. That doll is undoubtedly more effective than birth control.

I've been told that Sarah and her counterpart, blankie, carry an offensive smell — one that's been described as a cross between a sock and bag of Doritos. Naturally this poses its challenges in serious relationships that involve shared nights and sleeping spaces. I have found that my exes with sleep apnea or sinus disorders have been most accepting of my plus-one. Their sleep machines and excess mucus seem to mask Sarah's scent that, though revolting to most, is so comforting to me. Unfortunately for me, these sleep conditions are seldom referenced in dating bios.

that doll is

more effective

than birth control

ingredients

1.5 oz   Dewar's 12
.5 oz   Coffee-infused Bacardi Black
.5 oz   Marshmallow Syrup
2 dash   Bittercube Corazon bitters

garnish

Torched marshmallows

mixing instructions

In a mixing glass, add the Dewar's 12, coffee-infused Bacardi Black, marsh-mallow syrup & Bittercube Corazon bitters. Fill the mixing glass with ice. Stir the cocktail to chill & dilute. Strain the cocktail into a rocks glass over a single XL Cube. Garnish & enjoy.

(Tip)sy

For enhanced boozy flavor & pyrotechnics, soak your torched marshmallow skewer in Bacardi Black before burning. Use a high degree of caution.

the

s'morening
after

virgini-tease

I CLUNG TO MY VIRGINITY WITH AN UNYIELDING GRIP.

Riddled with pubescent insecurity, the threat of teen pregnancy was enough to scare me out of any high school rendezvous … as was the thought of getting naked in front of a boy. My decision to padlock my chastity belt and throw away the key was largely fear based. And though these anxieties alone overrode any peer pressures, I ultimately held off because every part of me believed (and still does!) that the first time is meant to be special.

Candles would be lit, sheets clean, and the night shared with my one true love — the high school quarterback. He would be sweet, I would be confident, and despite it being both of our first times, we would move in perfect unison to the J. Holiday lyrics that accompanied our naked duet. Next to prom night, it would be the most romantic and monumental evening of our young lives — surpassed only by our wedding and the birth of our two children years later.

As it turns out, my school didn't have a football team. And I didn't have sex in high school, let alone prom night. Instead I waited. And waited. And waited. And waited in my impenetrable prudishness for some semblance of the life-altering moment I longed for.

Then, at the ripe age of 20, it happened … ish.

is this what i

There was no music, just the applause of two bodies clapping together. There were no candles, just two lit, but consensual sophomores. There was no love, just unrequited lust. It was nothing romantic. Nothing monumental. Nothing special. Nothing at all like the perfect night I had etched in my virginal mind.

I woke up the next morning anticipating a rush of either regret or wisdom. In the many years I had to overthink "the morning after" my emotions were nothing like what I had expected. I wasn't embarrassed. I wasn't wiser. And surprisingly, I wasn't guilt ridden. Instead I felt nothing. And that didn't sit well with me.

Was sex supposed to feel like this? Like nothingness? Is this was I waited for? Is this IT?

waited for?

is *this* it?

Alongside tampons (check) and padded bras (check, check), I thought the act of sex would officially welcome me into the holy trinity of womanhood. I figured experiencing all three pillars of femininity would somehow earn me the sexy, unwavering female confidence that Aretha Franklin sings about. But it earned me nothing more than a hangover.

I sat up in my bed, reached for my water, and caught a glimpse of my half-naked self in the mirror. My once slicked-back pony was now in complete disarray. Nevertheless, I was proud that my drunken self was coherent enough to wash my face when I got home, before tucking myself into bed. Perhaps I was maturing after all?

My phone buzzed. It was him.

Before opening the message I thought about what I wanted him to say. I contemplated what I needed from him. Did I need anything at all? Could he say anything right now that would somehow alter this feeling of nothingness, making it somethingness? And would that somethingness become the pinnacle moment that catapults me into this virginal clinginess I hear about?

I sipped my water. I read his text.

It followed what I can only assume is post-hookup protocol. He thanked me for coming, said he had a good time, then he asked if he could buy a piece of ID off me. I looked just like his underage sister.

Is this standard? I wondered.

I wholeheartedly believe that sex is best with someone you love. While I have no regrets in my v-card's transaction. I know it would have meant more had that night been shared with someone I cared more deeply about and who. in turn. cared more deeply about me.

dryspells

ingredients

2.5 oz.'s Grey Goose
.5 oz.'s Noilly Prat sec
3 dash Orange bitters
        Fino Sherry rinse

garnish

a lemon twist

mixing instructions

Chill a martini glass with ice (unless you're serving over dry ice like all the cool kids do). In a mixing glass, add the Grey Goose, Noilly Prat sec & orange bitters. Fill the mixing glass with ice & stir the cocktail to chill & add dilution. Remove the ice from your chilled martini glass & rinse the glass with Fino Sherry. Strain the cocktail into the glass, garnish and serve.

Tipsy

Handle dry ice like a first string varsity athlete… with caution. Sure it's impressive to look at but get toooooo close & you may get severely burned.

grande dark roast

It was late February/early March and it was gloomy grey and bitter cold.

The only thing drier than my skin, or sense of humour, was the drought that stalked my love-less life.

After about two months of app downloading and binge-dating, I was in serious need of a hiatus. I had been on enough first dates to garner a "serial dater" rep, and I was beginning to believe that every guy on a dating app wanted one of two things: to marry you, immediately, or to bang you, also immediately. I wanted neither — least of all a stranger's genitals anywhere near me. So in an effort to clear both my mind and phone storage, I rid myself of Tinder, Bumble, and OkCupid.

every guy on a datin

to marr
imm

or to bang
imm

wanted one of two things:

you.

edtiately.

you.

ediately.

At first, the silence was welcomed! I enjoyed not being asked if my family had a history of male pattern baldness or if I wanted to break a headboard. But eventually, I became so single that I didn't even have anyone to fulfill my drunken textual desires — and that's a sobering realization that causes a girl to stop and reflect.

I was acutely aware of my singleness in more ways than one, which caused me to redefine "dry spells" in this modern dating world. Dry spells no longer seemed exclusive to a lack of intimacy, but in broader terms, referred to the absence of love interest in general. We live in a world where butt taps and double taps are of equal value and at that point I was getting neither. As much as I missed hand holding and makeout sessions, I craved WiFi butterflies — the butterflies you get when Mr. Right-Swipe pops up in your messages, or likes your latest photo. Despite my longings, I knew I needed a break from the window-shopping ways of app dating. I stood firm in my position and committed to my dating detox.

That's when I walked into my local coffee shop.

As the barista rhymed off my anthem-long drink order, I walked towards the counter with my eyes (naturally) glued to my phone. I blindly reached for my high-maintenance latte but instead bumped the hand of a man who at the same time turned swiftly, sending his hot coffee flying, right onto me. This handsome Anthony (as his cup read) apologized profusely and handed me a stack of napkins. It seemed inappropriate to ask him to pat me dry, though admittedly it crossed my mind.

I assured him I would survive and made some lame small talk about dry cleaning being a mere fraction of what a latte costs these days. He smiled politely. Insisting that he pay for my next full cup of coffee, he asked for my number. While I wished I had a profile to review before committing, I gave it to him, just like the olden days, and we made plans to see each other the following week.

He texted me later that day, which gave me a just a hint of those WiFi butter-flies! He apologized again and I smiled to myself. Inconvenience aside, a part of me felt compelled to thank him. Though tall dark roasts aren't my typical order (and I don't mean the coffee) this was the hottest things had gotten for me in a while.

this was the

hottest

things had gotten for me in awhile.

ingredients

2 oz	Bacardi Superior
3 oz	Fresh Honeydew Melon
.75 oz	Lemon juice
.5 oz	Simple syrup
.5 oz	Butterfly-pea flower syrup

garnish

Something new, borrowed & blue

mixing instructions

In a blender, add the Bacardi superior, fresh honeydew, lemon juice & simple syrup. Add one full 18 oz. mixing tin of ice to the blender & blend until smooth. Add the butterfly-pea flower syrup to a rocks glass & top with the blended cocktail. Finish with a cocktail umbrella, paper straw & drink up buttercup!

Tip/syp

Use extra Butterfly-pea flower syrup for that mandatory something blue!

i dew

something borrowed

FOR QUITE A WHILE I SUBSCRIBED TO THE BELIEF that times have changed—that more and more millennials had placed marriage on the backburner in exchange for travelling, career building and prolonged fuckboy-ing.

"Everyone's doing it," I decided, naively. It was a sad, albeit necessary rationale for my single state.

But in May 2016, this all changed.

In a matter of one weekend, my one friend got married, another engaged, while a third set the date for her nuptials. Suddenly my singleness seemed amplified and I felt robbed of the five to eight year buffer I had allotted myself.

With my parents' 30th wedding anniversary approaching, along with my 24th birthday—the same age my mom was when they got married—I spiralled into what I self-diagnosed as Jordan's quarter-life crisis.

While I was legitimately, whole-heartedly, elated for all three of my childhood friends, it did feel a little like getting punched, then slapped and then spat on in succession. Still, it wasn't until I received the save-the-date for my friend's wedding that I had officially declared myself doomed.

Once I saw past the matching plaid ensembles the happy couple was sporting, I noticed the bottom of the engagement photo read: August 5th, 2017.

My birthday.

In a humour only I can appreciate, I joked that my birthday could serve as this beautiful bride-to-be's something borrowed. The look on her face suggested that if I didn't immediately retract that statement, my pending bruises would be her something blue…so that's when I *uncharacteristically* closed my mouth, lest she revoke my plus-one.

Already discouraged that I may never matrimonially measure up to my parents' perfection, I gladly put the husband hunt on hold and instead focused my attention towards wedding date candidates.

Though a long-term boyfriend seemed entirely unreasonable given my track record, I most certainly could manage a lease for one evening. The thought of any relationship shorter-lived than an Instagram story was strangely anxiety releasing.

With my standards significantly dropped, suddenly I was less preoccupied with men's medical histories and/or how my first name sounded with their last. Instead, I was in search of someone who would pose willingly for a picture or two to my left; someone who could keep me conversationally engaged.

Poor choice of words…scratch that…interested. Someone who could keep me conversationally interested; and ultimately, someone who wouldn't judge my abuse of the presumed open bar.

Do you care for another? He'll ask.

I Do.

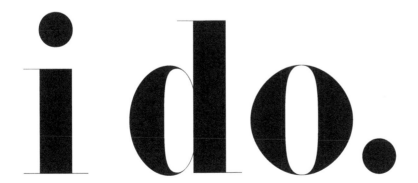

ginger *snap*

ingredients

1.5 oz	Cazadores Reposado
.5 oz	Benedictine
.5 oz	Ginger Syrup
.75 oz	Lime Juice
3 oz	Perrier

garnish

Dehydrated citrus & a mint sprig

mixing instructions

In a mule cup, add the Cazadores Reposado, Benedictine, ginger syrup & lime juice. Fill the cup with ice & stir the ingredients to mix evenly. Top with Perrier & stir again gently to mix. Top with more crushed ice, garnish and enjoy.

Tip/syp

The drink is chill. The ginger is not.
You've been warned.

red *solo*

BACK IN GRADE TEN my science teacher told our class that being a ginger was a birth defect. Right then, twenty sets of eyes turned to face me. The lone ginger. My face was undoubtedly more red than my hair. Thank you, Mr. Park. In that moment it became clear that an inability to tan and a love for a boy with whom I shared a name were the least of my worries: I was a soulless birth defect.

I carried that vulnerability with me through my high school days and well into my love and dating life. More often than not, I felt that my ginger handicap left me datingly-disadvantaged — as though my mane placed me well below my more highly sought after blonde and brunette counterparts.

Did my hair serve as a warning label, warding off potential suitors? Did my inability to tan deem me unsuitable arm candy? Were my fiery locks somehow indicative of the fiery temper within?

Enter dating apps.

Fearful that the red may lead to premature left swipes, I opted for a black and white lead photo for my first profile. I leaned instead on a witty bio, infectious smile, and my dog, hoping to garner a few right swipes before revealing my mane misfortunes to the men of Tinder and Bumble.

The results were staggering. While photos two to five may have read proceed with caution for some, they drew others in, like a moth to a flame. My people. In the depths of the iCloud I had uncovered what appeared to be a kingdom of ginger lovers, each expressing their admiration for my full coloured photos. With a new inspired confidence, I felt like their porcelain queen wearing my crown of enviable red hair. They were my suitors, all vying for a chance at love with this modern day Sansa Stark. I went from feeling like the rejected and defected to the fairest and rarest.

Oh if Mr. Park could see me now, I thought.

But upon agreeing to a date with one of these ginger lovers I was swiftly kicked off my high horse. Tall, handsome, and smart, he presented himself online as a latter-day knight in shining armour. It took two dates to conclude that he was really just a prick in tin foil.

The date was doomed from the start. Any points earned by opening my car door were quickly revoked when I learned he had put our reservation under Mr. & Mrs. As we followed the host to our dimly-lit table for two, I felt compelled to clarify that we were merely walking to our seats, and not down an aisle. There seemed to be some confusion, but I bit my tongue.

Despite my best efforts to turn the dying date around, I decided the night was unsalvageable once he insisted on discussing the medical histories of both my maternal and paternal sides. I was about ready to fake-faint my way out of the remainder of the evening, but just as I got into character, fanning myself profusely with my napkin, my charming date's next words nearly knocked me off my chair. No fainting required.

"If not for the male pattern baldness in your family, you would be a prime candidate for my wife," he told me.

The look of horror across my face didn't silence him.

He continued, "With that red hair and those green eyes, our children would certainly take on my dominant features."

Suddenly his nose seemed rather large, and his hands rather small. Talk about a birth defect.

As he proceeded to list his many accolades, all of which he hoped to pass of to his future offspring, I decided that I was over his misogyny and that I was not obligated to sit here in a manner as passive as my recessive genes.

So as our server reappeared, not a moment too soon with our second round of drinks, I grabbed my glass before it even so much as touched the table. I threw back that pinot like a shot of vodka, placed it on the kind and confused server's tray, and sent back my date's glass of Chardonnay.

"He prefers the red," I said as I grabbed my jacket, bag and left.

no fainting required

he prefers

the red

ingredients

1.5 oz	Grey Goose Ducasse
.75 oz	Crème de cacao
1 oz	Freshly brewed espresso
2 dash	Bittercube Corazon bitters

garnish

Freshly shaved chocolate

mixing instructions

In a mixing tin, add the Grey Goose Ducasse, crème de cacao, freshly brewed espresso & Corazon bitters. Fill the tin with ice & shake what your momma gave you. Double strain the cocktail into a chilled, small rocks glass. Garnish with freshly shaved chocolate & enjoy.... together!

Tipsy

For a drink that will keep the two of you you up all night long, add another half ounce of espresso to this yummy nightcap!

dtf *down to fudge*

the alcoholidays

HOLIDAYS ARE DESIGNED FOR COUPLES. Fireworks, mistletoe, midnights, even costumes are all made better with a significant other. The greatest offender, of course, is Valentine's Day.

In primary school, I loved February 14th.

In a time before text messaging, Valentine's Day was a rare opportunity to confess, through the written word, a budding love for a classmate. It was also one of the few days of the year this redhead could wear pink. And so, with the sparkliest of gel pens and the highest of hopes, I would replace the impersonal *from* with *love*, on my crush's card, then proudly sign my name with exes and ohs. I would seal his holographic Valentine with an extra Hershey Kiss, to ensure his was a standout among the rest. Then I'd slide his custom card into his paper bag mailbox, the throwback equivalent to today's DMs, and wait for him to love me back.

If the gesture was well received and the feelings mutual, which was the case in grades one to three, my crush would invite me to join him in the infamous Love Pit at recess. Situated on the top of the primary yard hill, the Love Pit overlooked the entire playground. It was a large, round hole of dirt that our primary predecessors dug up before us. The hole served many purposes but was used most commonly for our recess weddings. In that pit the bride and groom would stand, surrounded by friends from both sides, and commit their *love* for each other with a hug. Once hugged out, the new couple was bound to one another at least until the next day.

And it was as easy as that. That's when Valentine's Day was fun. When a pile of dirt and pink tulle skirt were thrill enough and before I actually knew what lust, or worse, love felt like. Since adding real love to my emotional repertoire I've become acutely aware of Valentine's Day's cruel placement in the calendar year, especially when single. When people say it's better to have loved and lost than to never have loved at all, they mustn't be factoring in the holidays.

By the time gloomy February rolls around, the lonely in love just survived an entire season of songs, commercials and dinner deals dedicated to holiday romance. We endured two months of mitten-embraced lovers and pyjama-coordinated couples spamming our newsfeeds, with their generic photos and captions. And though we may have given out a few obligatory double-taps here and there, I have to believe that the majority of us Single Bells really just didn't give two turtledoves.

Those of us who make it through a mistletoe-less December and a smooch-less New Year have earned the right to celebrate our perseverance through an equal opportunity holiday—one that relationship status needn't define. But before we can party in a matter akin to St. Patrick, the calendar insists on adding insult to injury and piercing our already broken hearts with Cupid's dull arrow.

I try to approach Valentine's Day with the same enthusiasm and positivity that I did two decades ago, with a heart less burdened by love's defeat. I don't often succeed. Admittedly, single or otherwise, my February 14th's have been on a slow albeit steady decline since elementary school. There was however one exception.

The day started off with a surprise flower delivery. Twelve red roses arrived at my doorstep with a sweet handwritten card. It shared his excitement for dinner that evening and asked if I'd be his Valentine. With the date already in my Google calendar, I politely re-accepted.

When we arrived at the location, we rode the elevator up thirty-eight floors where the doors opened to a dimly lit space with exceptional views of Toronto's lakefront. For a moment, I thought of the Love Pit and remembered back to the time that sad pile of dirt overlooking the schoolyard felt like the top of the world. Both the wine and conversations were flowing. We sat for nearly three hours through a five-course meal before making our way back to his place.

The perfect gentleman, he opened the front door for me and took my coat before handing me a stemless glass of wine. We toasted to a wonderful night and moved further into his apartment, where he revealed the third surprise of the night—a large box of chocolates and Valentine's Day card. Though still full from dinner, he insisted I open the heart-shaped box. Never one to turn down a sweet, I obliged. Inside, surrounded by chocolates, was a tinier blue box which held a pair of crystal earrings. For the second time in one day I was rendered speechless. Never had I felt so special and spoiled by someone other than my parents. Tears of equal parts shock and gratitude started rolling down my cheeks as he handed me the card.

I read what I could with my tear-blurred eyes, sniffling relentlessly at every sweet word, right to the very end where the impersonal from was scratched out and replaced with love. Then he signed his name, with exes and ohs.

with x's and o's.

nudi tea

ingredients

2 oz	Green Tea Infused Bombay Sapphire Gin
.75 oz	Lemon Juice
.75 oz	Ginger Syrup
2-3	Slices of Fresh Cucumber
1 tsp	Matcha Powder
1 oz	Perrier

garnish

Cucumber ribbons

mixing instructions

In a mixing tin, add the fresh cucumber slices & muddle them. Next add the green tea-infused Bombay Sapphire & matcha powder. Stir the powder into the gin & cucumber to mix it evenly & prevent any clumping. Add the lemon juice & ginger syrup before filling the tin with ice. Shake the cocktail vigorously… & I mean VIGOROUSLY. Triple strain the cocktail to remove any unwanted matcha clumps & pour into a Collins glass over ice. Top with Perrier, garnish and enjoy!

Tipsy

Try this cocktail recipe without the green tea gin for a refreshingly tasty matcha mocktail that's socially acceptable to drink at any hour of the day!

10

unsolicid*ck

As inspired by your unrequested dick pic, I'm going to keep this chapter short.

Apparently mixtapes and love letters are out, and unsolicited dick pics are in. Like an unstoppable computer virus, misleadingly angled and poorly filtered photos, are sweeping smartphones of female users everywhere — single or otherwise. We are in desperate need of some anti-virus protection. As these unwarranted photos reveal themselves in my Instagram inbox, I question what compels a man, such as yourself, to send such a thing unprovoked.

ridick

What is going through your head? (And I am referring to the one north of the belt buckle … with the supposed brain inside.)

Do you realize that this image is a throwback to flashing? Do you understand that posing with an inanimate object, like a remote, radiates insecurity? And are you aware that - like herpes - this dic-ture is the "gift" that will keep on giving? Gentlemen, for every unsolicited dick pic you send, assume it has been seen

ulous.

by no less than five other sets of eyes. The general consensus? We would rather poke fun at it than be poked by it.

And so, I anxiously await the day these "smartphones" of ours are finally smart enough to filter that which some men, like yourself, cannot.

Ridickulous.

ingredients

1.5 oz	Bombay Sapphire
.5 oz	Martini Bianco
.5 oz	Coconut Water Syrup
.75 oz	Lime Juice
1 tsp	Maca Powder
1.5 oz	Martini Prosecco

the Turn

mixing instructions

In a mixing tin, add the Bombay Sapphire, Martini Bianco, coconut water syrup, lime juice & maca powder. Stir the maca powder until blended evenly with the liquid. Fill the tin with ice & shake vigorously to dilute and chill. Double strain the cocktail into a light bulb shaped glass & top with Martini prosecco. Add a paper straw & enjoy.

Tipsy

This cocktail is all about presentation! While we have backlit this cocktail & edited in post for effect, you can recreate this neon drink using submersive LED lights (it's a thing. Google it). Serve, & get lit!

oh

it's

11

scentual

My memory is often jogged by my heightened sense of smell.

To this day, the faintest whiff of Axe instantly transports me back to my Catholic high school cafeteria *by day*, turned unofficial raunchy, underage nightclub. In a similar sense, the smell of VEX or Malibu rum sparks elusive memories of every school dance thereafter.

Having a nose akin to that of a pregnant woman or dog presents its challenges for the single girl. Just as some eat with their eyes, I most certainly date with my nose. When a kiss or embrace is met with a stiff whiff of bad breath or B.O., I'm instantly turned off with no room for recovery. In my humble opinion, those who do not practice safe breath are most effectively practising safe sex. As in there's no way they're having sex…right?

i'm not

Not surprisingly, smemory—smell memory—is how I namelessly categorize the men of my dating past.

Most notably, there was All Gas No Class—A Jimmy Neutron look-alike, who took a laxative before a three-hour road trip without the manners to excuse himself. Then there was Mr. Stench Press—A Ken doll look-alike, who believed in two-a-day workouts and twice-a-week showers. While my eyes could appreciate his dedication, my nose most certainly could not.

For obvious reasons, these romances were short-lived as was any encounter with a gentleman doused in the same cologne as my ex. Viktor&Rolf Spicebomb, you have forever been ruined for me. Gain laundry detergent and Mahogany Teakwood candles, you've been exiled as well.

As a single woman, it's discouraging to know that no matter how thoroughly I analyze a match's profile or how diligently I research him beyond the limits of the app, one of the most important questions remains unanswered:

What does he smell like?

Currently, this is a question that can only be answered through the inconvenience of trial and error. Dear reader, I do believe that many an hour of worthless small talk and awkward dates could have been spared if dating apps offered a scratch-and-sniff feature. Only then could I all-knowingly swipe, sift, and sniff my way to love.

But I'm not holding my breath.

holding my breath.

ingredients

1.5 oz	Bombay Sapphire
.75 oz	Rosemary syrup
.75 oz	Lemon juice
3-4	Fresh Blackberries
1.5 oz	Martini Prosecco

garnish

Clothespinned torched rosemary

mixing instructions

In a mixing tin muddle the fresh blackberries. Add the Bombay Sapphire, rosemary syrup & lemon juice. Fill the tin with ice & (you guessed it) shake vigorously to dilute and chill. Double strain the cocktail into a chilled coupe & top with Prosecco. Garnish & share with your perfect match.

(Tip)sy

For an impressive presentation, torch the rosemary sprig. Create photographic evidence. Post to Instagram so it happened. Tag me. Put out flame. Serve.

the *perfect* match

12

i cloud
nine

GROWING UP, LONG SUMMER DRIVES WERE ALWAYS THE SAME.

My brother Parker, my sister Braedie and I, PB&J, would sandwich ourselves in the back, drowning in a sea of blankets, pillows and toys. A snack-packed cooler sat at my mom's feet, she'd hold up treats like a concession stand. As we drove for hours to one of our favourite getaways, a movie played in the back to pacify our impatience. My siblings' eyes stayed glued to the screen. Mine remained locked on our parents ahead.

hand-
in-
hand

Hand-in-hand, with their fingers intertwined, they'd rest their arms on the console between them. For a moment or two, my dad would take his eyes off the road, just to look at my mom. "You're beautiful, you know that?" He whispered. More often than not, she'd bashfully reject his compliment. "You are," he'd say, firm in his position and return his gaze to the road. Hands still embraced, he'd pull hers in closer and kiss right below her ring—the same ring he placed on her finger over thirty years ago.

For my parents, subtle moments of affection aren't exclusive to long drives; they're threaded throughout each and every day. These daily gestures, I infer, show that they've not only been married thirty-one years, but those thirty-one years have been spent happily and in love. With younger eyes these moments may have made me wince, but hearing my mom tell my dad she loves him, and seeing him smile and say it back, is a sound byte of my life I will never take for granted.

I hope one day to have what they have. But a part of me worries a love like theirs is as antiquated as dial-up internet, landlines, or Twitter. Sometimes, as I mindlessly swipe through a roster of Bumble men, too apathetic to read a full bio, I wonder if millennial hearts have the same short attention span as our minds. Are we capable of relationships worth spanning three decades? Can an app algorithm generate a love like theirs? Do any eligible men open doors anymore? Can we find our cloud nine in the ambiguous iCloud?

Discouraged, I close Bumble, but open Instagram soon after. Before I know it, I'm enthralled in a never-ending newsfeed of relationship competition and subconscious comparison. I scroll through countless photos of extravagant travels, anniversary celebrations, thoughtful date nights and engagement rings, and somehow deem these images the new standard.

My parents, free of all social media, are unphased by this. Their time together isn't spent scrolling through other people's lives, it's spent making their own— something the rest of us do between WiFi signals. When the workday is done, both my mom and my dad unplug so that by the time they sit down for dinner, no phone is in sight. Dinner has always been a time to talk about our days.

With three adult children now, the seats at our dinner table are not always full. Neither is the backseat of the car. But no matter which combination of the five of us are home, we all revert to our usual seat and enjoy a meal my mom makes, thoughtfully considering each of our ever-changing dietary needs.

"Don't forget to eat your vegetables," she encourages, as she looks over at my dad's otherwise clean plate. He's never enjoyed his greens.

"Might as well call them vege-terribles," he echoes back, before silencing his rebuttal with a forkful of peas and corn. He's always had substantially fewer veggies than the rest of us anyway. A compromise at its simplest and finest.

My dad looks left towards my mom. "You're beautiful, you know that?" He says.

As always, she modestly objects.

"You are."

psychotic

ingredients

2 oz.   Cazadores Reposado Tequila
1 oz   Grilled Pineapple Puree
.75 oz   Bird's Eye Chili Rich Simple Syrup Syrup
1 oz   Lime Juice

garnish

A single pineapple frond

mixing instructions

In a mixing tin, add the Cazadores Reposado, grilled pineapple puree, simple syrup & lime juice. Fill the tin with ice & shake vigorously, then strain the cocktail into a rocks glass over fresh ice. Garnish with a single pineapple frond (that's as single as you are) & voila!

(Tip)sy

Like your drinks like you like your men... on ice? Add cracked ice to your rock glass for a refreshing, slushie-like ice consistency!

13

the

buzz: **calling it quits**

I'VE EXPERIENCED HEARTBREAK TWICE IN MY LIFE—the first when I was twenty-three, the second when I was twenty-five. Much like the men and the relationships themselves, the breakups and subsequent recoveries were vastly different.

The first was like an unchased tequila shot—one that hit me hard, suddenly and hurt to swallow.

With a kitchen island between us, I stood at the counter while he sat at the table. For a moment I remembered sitting at that table together, my hand in his and he told me he loved me for the first time. It felt much different now. As I looked across at him and he looked back at me, I knew that despite our locked eyes, we no longer saw one another. We may have cared for each other, but we were certainly no longer in love.

His shaking leg and fidgety hands gave away what he was about to say, but my heart still sank the moment he told me it was over. It had been more than two years since we'd fallen in love and though I denied it for days thereafter, our love had run its course. He was able to admit it, but I wasn't ready to let go.

With wiser eyes, I look back now knowing I was holding on not out of love but out of fear—fear of being alone. He was my first love and I had foolishly convinced myself that I could not live without him, forgetting of course that I had done so for twenty years prior. But in the thick of it all, a day without a good morning text or a goodnight phone call seemed unfathomable.

The initial week apart moved slowly. I spent the majority of those days in bed, alone with issues and tissues, nursing my breakup hangover. As I lamented our two-and-a-half year relationship, I wished hopelessly that things could go back to the way they once were,—back to the Jeep days when we drove around, windows down, world off, listening to the country music I pretended to dislike so much. Little did he know that Zac Brown Band played on loop when we were apart, the songs reminding me of him and the lyrics tattooed on his back. In time, I came to realize I was grieving a relationship long-gone. The Jeep had since been sold for parts and the soundtrack no longer sounded quite as sweet. I continued to shed as many pounds as I did tears, relishing in the fact that my breakup was the best diet I had ever been on.

My second heartbreak was much different, dear reader. Unlike my previous tequila-shot split, where the breakup buzz was immediate and the recovery intense, my next split felt more like a residual hangover, one that spanned nearly six months—the last six months of our relationship.

At first, I blamed the meddlers—the group of people we allowed to permeate our relationship. I resented them for deluding our buzz with their myopic perspective and for offering up their unsolicited thoughts and opinions. I have since come to see that while they created cracks, it was he and I that created craters. If we had stood on a more solid foundation, perhaps we would have mended those fractures rather than making them bigger. Or if we loved each other as deep as we tried to convince ourselves we did, maybe we would have been unphased by the cracks altogether. Instead, our residual hangover ensued. It was nearly six months of talking rather than listening, winning instead of solving, liking but not loving. My emotions confused him. His walls angered me. Passion faded. Hope soon followed.

My first shot at love I was scared to admit we were growing apart, out of fear of being alone. My second shot at love I learned that being with someone doesn't make you immune from loneliness. So by the time my phone rang that Saturday morning, I too was ready to call it quits. There was no breakup buzz or hangover to combat. If anything, I finally felt sober.

i finally felt sober

four *play*

ingredients

.75 oz.	Bombay Sapphire
.75 oz	St-Germain
.75 oz	Martini Riserva Speciale Ambrato
.75 oz	Lemon Juice

garnish

A lemon twist

mixing instructions

In a mixing tin, add the Bombay Sapphire, St-Germain, Martini Riserva Speciale Ambrato & lemon juice. Fill the tin with ice & shake your groove thing, shake your groove thing yeah, yeah (show 'em how we do it now). Double strain the cocktail into a chilled coupe, garnish & enjoy.

Tipsy

Find out what you like... experiment! You can create your own variation of a "Fourplay" cocktail using different combinations of spirit, liqueur, vermouth and fruit juice. Just ensure all parts are equal... like any good Fourplay.

14

queen of hearts

By now I'm sure it is clear, dear reader, that on the subjects of love, dating and relationships, I am a 100% certified non-expert.

If you subscribe to Gladwell's 10,000 Rule, a theory which suggests that ten thousand deliberate hours of practice can make you an expert in any field, I should be a master dater by now. In adding up my hours of swiping, small talk, dates and writing this book, I am surely at or nearing that ten thousand hour mark. But beyond the personal anecdotes sketched across these pages, I suppose I have little to show for it.

So let's call a spade a spade—I am certainly not a relationship pro. Any ex of mine will attest to that. As you have read, I didn't start off particularly proficient at the whole single thing either. I played games. I took risks where I shouldn't have. I got scared when the stakes got high. I showed my cards too soon. I folded when I had a really great hand. So believe me, given my track record, the irony of me penning a dating book is not lost on me, but I've become more adept. Though I wouldn't call myself a player, I'm most certainly learning the game.

What I do know is that love is polarizing. At this point in time, the only thing I fear more than falling in love is never falling in love again. Go figure. I've had love. I (at times) took it for granted. I've lost it. And it hurt. It hurt a lot. Have I recovered? Absolutely! And quicker than I thought possible. But undoubtedly, at the end of any once meaningful relationship, there is bound to be that residual damage, which onward takes the form of insecurities, trust issues, or just plain fear—fear that you'll once again be dealt the same unsuccessful hand.

But don't fold on love, dear reader. If there is anything I hope you to take from this book, it's just that. Despite the many ups and downs of this modern dating world, I believe wholeheartedly that the risk is worth the reward.

Today's technology adds layers of both excitement and anxiety for the modern dating girl. I enjoy seeing how people choose to present themselves in a matter of six photos and a character limited bio. I like getting to know someone that catches my eye online and seeing if we can build a banter capable of withstanding a drink in the real world. Having that initial iCloud space between myself and my matches also makes for an easy exit if necessary. On these terms, I am confident and unapologetically me.

But these apps have their blinders. When sifting through a day's matches, I turn a blind eye to the fact that I'm not the only one with access to this roulette of eligible men. Though I don't see them, there are other matches being made, conversations being had and other women in play. It isn't until after date three, four or five with a promising gentleman that I'm reminded of dating apps' window shopping ways.

Is he still swiping? I wonder. Should I be? I don't really want to. Is it too soon to feel that way? Certainly too soon to ask, right? I dunno…our dates have been great. I bet he deleted the app at this point. Though, he didn't message me much last night. Probably on another date. I should probably have a glass of wine.

For me, with budding feelings comes insecurity, and shortly thereafter over-thinking rears its ugly head. And while this is my Achilles' heel in love, I have learned that we all have our relationship drawbacks. We all wear our poker faces. In fact dating has a tendency at times to feel like a large deck of people, all lost in the shuffle, seeing each other's abandonment issues and raising one another a paralyzing fear of commitment. It's the one who calls your bluff, and goes all in, regardless of the hands you've both been dealt—that's when you know you've met your match. And maybe, just maybe, I've met mine.

you've **met** *your* **match.**

acknowledgements

Mom & Daddy, I believe in love because of you two. Thank you for your unwavering support and encouragement in all my endeavours. A book is far easier to write when you're backed by people who believe in you more than you believe in yourself at times. I love you both tremendously.

Braedie & Parker, I'm sorry if you have learned far more than you've ever cared to about your big sister. The Peanut and Butter to my Jelly, I love you both. #PB&J

Kris & Bacardi Canada, I cannot thank you enough for being excited about this project! You have been such a breeze and a blessing to work with. Your creativity is both insane and delicious! You are a true artist and I'm honoured to have worked with you.

Olivia, the first to hop on the korskCREWed train… and boy am I happy you came aboard! Thank you for your enthusiasm and your unparalleled expertise. Without you this gorgeous book would be bound with staples and printed in Times New Roman. Size 12 font. Minus titles. Your work is stunning and you have such a bright future ahead of you. I so appreciate your attention to detail and your commitment to making my thoughts tangible, and more beautiful than I could imagine.

Bri, I'm, sorry, for, the, commas. Thanks for cutting them down. You really have been an "exclamation mark" in this whole process! Your energy is contagious and uplifting and really helped propel this whole thing forward. I truly appreciate how excited you've been about bringing these stories to life. I also love that you think I'm funny.

Paige, thank you for reading through this book in its early stages and offering up your invaluable suggestions! I'm grateful you encouraged me to dive deeper into each story and share more detail with my reader. This book wouldn't be the same without your eye!

Elaine, it was a pleasure getting to work with you again, this time on a project of my own. Thank you for capturing these cocktails and introducing me to Kris. This is a great example of how sliding into someone's DM's can actually pay off from time to time.

Emily, Emily, Emily. Talk about things coming full circle, eh? You knew me through the bulk of these chapters and it seemed only fitting to work with you on my author photo. It was such a pleasure working with you in your element. You are a true talent and a true friend. Whether it was in university or through this book process, thank you for always capturing the moments that I sometimes forget to live in! I'm so proud of you.

Laura, it felt just like a classic Western pre-drink preparing 15+ cocktails in your kitchen! Cannot thank you enough for lending me your beautiful space to shoot the cocktails for this book. I only wish you could have played hooky from work and taste-tested each of them with me.

To the men in this book, it would be unfair to paint you all with the same brush. Some of you are wonderful. Some of you suck. I'm thankful for you no matter which category you fall into. You helped me grow. Thanks for the stories.

To my future husband, call me. Or slide into my DM's. Or whatever.

To you, dear reader, for purchasing this book and reading right to the very end.

jordan quinn

Toronto. 26. Leo. Non-smoker. Non-vegan.
Western Grad. Small Business Owner.
Likes long walks on the beach, while wearing SPF 50.
And now, a published Author.

CPSIA information can be obtained
at www.ICGtesting.com
Printed in the USA
LVHW021345180119
604312LV00003B/6/P